30 N
... Be
Driv

CW00820575

30 Minutes

... Before Your Driving Test

Edward Baker
with Peter Dore

KOGAN
PAGE

YOURS TO HAVE AND TO HOLD

BUT NOT TO COPY

First published in the UK by Kogan Page, 1998

Kogan Page Limited
120 Pentonville Road
London N1 9JN

British Library Cataloguing in Publication Data
A CIP record for this book is available from the British Library.

ISBN 0 7494 2521 0

Typeset by The Florence Group, Stoodleigh, Devon
Printed and bound in Great Britain by Clays Ltd, St Ives plc

CONTENTS

The 30 Minutes Series

The *Kogan Page 30 Minutes Series* has been devised to give your confidence a boost when faced with tackling a new skill or challenge for the first time.

So the next time you're thrown in at the deep end and want to bring your skills up to scratch or pep up your career prospects, turn to the *30 Minutes Series* for help!

Titles available are:

30 Minutes Before Your Job Interview
30 Minutes Before a Meeting
30 Minutes Before a Presentation
30 Minutes to Boost Your Communication Skills
30 Minutes to Brainstorm Great Ideas
30 Minutes to Deal with Difficult People
30 Minutes to Succeed in Business Writing
30 Minutes to Master the Internet
30 Minutes to Make the Right Decision
30 Minutes to Make the Right Impression
30 Minutes to Plan a Project
30 Minutes to Prepare a Job Application
30 Minutes to Write a Business Plan
30 Minutes to Write a Marketing Plan
30 Minutes to Write a Report
30 Minutes to Write Sales Letters

Available from all good booksellers.
For further information on the series, please contact:

Kogan Page, 120 Pentonville Road, London N1 9JN
Tel: 0171 278 0433 Fax: 0171 837 6348

INTRODUCTION

Take a glance at the shelves of any high-street bookshop and you'll find dozens of titles on how to pass the test, all packed with a dizzying amount of technical information. This book isn't.

The view taken here is that almost everything that you need in order to pass your test should be supplied by an Approved Driving Instructor or ADI. Books can supplement this input but can never replace an instructor's warmth, common sense and moral guidance.

So why another book? The answer is simple: fear. This book is about how you can overcome and use that fear to pass that test!

1

GETTING STARTED

The good news
and the bad news

Let's start with the bad news. More than half of the would-be drivers taking their test are going to fail. Some will fail spectacularly, some by the slimmest of margins; some will fail on their first attempt, some after many attempts. In the end, however, the result is just the same. A failure is a failure is a failure. And it hurts.

The good news, however, is that you don't have to be

Table 1 The odds against you

Year	Pass rate
94/95	46.90%
95/96	45.71%
96/97	44.73%

(Source DSA)

one of them! There are measures that you can take and attitudes that you can adopt to significantly tip the odds in your favour. All you have to do is use them.

It's worth reflecting on the fact that the same four ingredients go to make up a test pass or failure. The four ingredients, in rising order of importance, are as follows:

1. the examination

2. the examiner

3. the instructor

4. the candidate.

Note carefully where the buck stops with this particular view of test performance. It stops with the candidate – with you.

The examination

The most important thing to remember about your driving test is this – there are no surprises in it!

There is nothing, absolutely nothing, in this thirty minute examination of mental and physical skills that you will not have encountered already if you have prepared well. The examiner will ask you to duplicate a series of activities laid down in the current edition of *The Driving Test* published by Her Majesty's Stationery Office. Activities that you should have practised many times before.

It is equally important to understand how you will be marked during the test. Examiners are taught to look for the perfect drive, whilst accepting that they are not very likely to find it. Because of this, a few 'minor faults' are acceptable. You need to be aware of this all through your test. It may seem like the end of the world to you, but to the examiner it's only a small error. Ignore it, proceed to the next manoeuvre and pass! Do you know how many minor faults you are allowed during a test? If you don't know, find out now. And having found out, repeat that magic number over and over again until you can feel and believe it inside. The confidence that can be gained from accepting that you do not need to be perfect is immeasurable.

The examiner

The second key ingredient in the test is the examiner who will test you. It's important that you understand just what an examiner is.

Driving examiners are not made in hell, but in a place called Cardington. Here, individuals from all over are rigorously trained to pass or fail candidate drivers according to a nationally agreed standard.

To become a driving examiner a person must satisfy the following requirements:

- He or she must have held a clean driving licence for a minimum of five years.

- He or she must be over twenty-five and under fifty-seven years of age at the commencement of training.

- He or she must be a good communicator.

This list hasn't been made in order to belittle examiners, but to demythologize them. They are not a special breed of human being with superhuman skill levels and degrees in mental torture. They are just people doing their job. And that job is by no means an easy one. Driving examiners have to put up with a lot of grief from members of the public who 'should' have passed their tests. They have to listen to and put up with insults, tears, and occasional threats from people who have been told by their husband, wife, brother or dog that they are really good. The fact that they went through several sets of lights, almost mowed down a pedestrian and broke several land speed records is lost on them. The examiner is unfair, sneaky and, of course, wrong.

Try to rid yourself of any preconceptions that you may have about the fairness of the examination and the examiners.

The instructor

'Anyone' can teach you to drive, but not necessarily to test standards. The distinction is an important one. There's little point in making lots of effort only to discover that you have been working to the wrong set of rules. That's why finding the right person to teach you is such a big issue. The person best equipped to deliver tuition in this life-and-death skill is someone qualified as an Approved Driving Instructor or ADI. An ADI is a man or woman who has spent both a great deal of time and money in order to pass three very difficult examinations. At the end of this process the successful applicants are granted a green badge, which is effectively their licence to teach.

A glance at the telephone directory will reveal a bewildering variety of driving instructors to choose from. The best way to find an instructor, however, is by personal introduction. Ask your friends or colleagues who they recommend. The chances are that if the ADI did a proper job for them he or she will do the same for you.

If you genuinely can't find an instructor this way then you will need to start shopping around. The 'item' that you are buying may end up costing several hundred pounds, so it's important to have a clear idea of what you want for your money. Ring a selection of schools and ask the following questions:

- What is the status of the ADI (full licence or trainee)?

- What study aids or lesson plans are provided?

- How many pupils will be in the car?

- How many lessons are recommended for someone of your experience?

- How much do individual lessons cost and are there any discounts for block booking?

- What happens in the event of test failure?

You should pay particular attention to the last point. A few schools offer a 'guaranteed pass' which is both illegal and illogical. As you have already seen, the chances of any individual passing the test are less than fifty per cent. If an instructor offered free and unlimited tuition to every failure, he or she would soon end up working for nothing! Clarify what the offers mean in concrete terms and be wary of something that sounds too good to be true. It usually is.

Having narrowed the field down, you should go out on a few trial lessons or assessments. These are usually free, or charged at a reduced rate so you can afford to be choosy. Your instructor will be evaluating you, but you should also be evaluating him or her. All sorts of things that might seem trivial at first can become real pains given time and pressure. For example, the instructor might smoke or have a sarcastic sense of humour, which initially might seem acceptable but might become distracting and irritating. Take time over your selection of an instructor. You are making an important and expensive investment. Get it right.

Finally, there are some things that you should not expect from an ADI. Any instructor who snaps at you or bullies you should be dispensed with at once. The problem of the 'overly tactile' instructor is mainly encountered by female pupils and needs to be tackled at once. There is absolutely no reason why anyone teaching you how to drive has to touch you in order to do so. If this occurs, or if suggestive talk is introduced as a way of making you 'relax', change schools as soon as possible and report the offender to the DSA.

The candidate

The exam, the examiner and the instructor are not the most important part of the test equation. That honour belongs to the candidate.

Because most people drive, there is a tendency to treat driving as an entitlement rather than something that has to be learnt. A little knowledge picked up here and there adds to this dismissive air.

Go into your test with such an attitude and you are more than likely to fail. To learn such an exacting skill as driving, you will have to work hard. That means that you will need to turn up for lessons on time, practise your skills, even though you think you know it all, and spend some money too.

As you add up the mounting cost of tuition, books and other things, you may feel that it is very expensive. But this is only thinking in the short term. You are 'buying' something that will last you the rest of your life. Even if it costs you around four hundred pounds to pass your test, how much is that worked out per day if you plan to drive for the next thirty years? The cost is ridiculously small if you look at it that way.

How to use this book

Read this book carefully from cover to cover. Decide which parts apply to you and then act, gathering together any resources you need (other books, special kinds of training, etc). Take an active part in designing your tuition from the start. When you get to the test you'll be sitting it on your own, so get used to responsibility now.

2

SAFETY CHECKS

Why people fail their tests
(according to those who fail)

If you were to conduct a poll amongst those people who had just failed their driving tests, you would more than likely come across the following explanations:

- My instructor was useless and taught me incorrectly.

- The examiner was useless and didn't like me because I'm young/old/black/white/male/female, etc.

- The test centre was useless and has a lousy pass rate.

- They have a quota system and I was unlucky enough to be over their daily quota.

- I can drive better than most of the people who've passed anyway.

Before looking at each of these excuses in turn it's worth stating for the record that they are just that – excuses.

If you have any baggage of this sort, get rid of it now. If you don't, then you are going to make the task that you are facing harder than it needs to be.

The first and most obvious person to blame for examination failure is the hapless instructor. In the time between waving the aspirant off and smiling sadly on return, he or she has often sprouted horns. This is a common, understandable, but usually unfair response. Scratch beneath the surface and you'll find that holders of this view are often on their third, fourth or more instructor. Is the DSA really allowing so many incompetents to teach without checking their performance? Or is there, perhaps, another reason?

The second target of an aggrieved candidate is generally the examiner. He, she, or it is prejudiced or biased and passed a friend last week who is a much worse driver! Once again, it's worth remembering that the DSA has standards for examiners and instructors as well as drivers. Anyone who made decisions on the basis of such attitudes would quickly find him or herself out of a job.

The Test Centre itself can also be made into a culprit. In areas where there are several to choose from, one quite often gets a bad reputation – the examiners are awkward, the pass rate is lower, etc. Then again, it might be the surrounding roads or roundabouts that are at fault. Beyond stating the obvious fact that to pass your test you should be competent enough to cope with reasonable conditions anywhere, common sense should also tell you that it would serve nobody to have such inconsistencies among test centres. Least of all would it help the DSA, who would find one centre mysteriously underbooked and unprofitable.

Another common myth is that 'they have a quota system' – 'they' being the DSA, who allegedly decide in advance how many candidates for the test are going to pass or fail each week. According to this view, it doesn't matter how good a driver you are. If you take your examination after the magic number has been reached, you're bound to fail. That's an excuse, too.

The most dangerous lie a test failure can tell him or herself is 'I can drive better than those who have already passed'. This point blank refusal to accept that there might be a problem with one's driving makes any further learning impossible. Should you be labouring under this particular delusion, then you need to do some serious thinking before you waste any more time or money. What those around you say is irrelevant, as is your own opinion of your abilities. What really matters is whether you can perform a laid out sequence of manoeuvres and exercises in a safe manner under reasonable conditions. If you can't do that, how can you claim to be a better driver than others on the road?

Why people fail their tests (according to the professionals)

The DSA, examiners and driving instructors all have a small, three-word explanation as to why more than fifty per cent of candidates fail their driving tests. It's this: *lack of preparation*. Read this again and accept it as a fact. Lack of preparation causes most failures and is therefore avoidable. Do you have trouble with a reverse park? If so, that's probably down to a lack of preparation. Is changing gear difficult? That comes down to a lack of practice, too. Whatever you choose to pick upon – lane discipline, speed control, roundabouts or whatever, it boils down to the same thing in the end.

The simple fact is that most people arrive at their test with insufficient training behind them. Eagerness to 'get it over with' or 'get going' leads to unrealistic expectations. If there is one sure way to tip the odds in favour of passing your test, then this is it. Prepare yourself and be guided by your instructor, not your emotional state. You may feel that you've practised enough, that there is nothing else to do, but you are not the best judge in this situation. Get as much practice in as you can.

Are you getting enough?

The success of your test attempt will be largely determined by the amount of training that you undertake beforehand. For reasons of cost and time, a great many people tend to 'ration' their time with a qualified instructor. Lessons are skipped, postponed or spread out over months or even years. Like many so-called economies, this can prove to be a false one.

Learning to drive isn't just a mental process like remembering names or theories, it's a *physical* process that requires a whole new range of conditioned reflexes, response times and hand to eye co-ordination skills. If you need to think about what you are doing it can often be too late.

It's also important that you have a structured plan of learning to stick to. Breaking off here and there will weaken your resolve, technique and cause you lots of other problems, so before you begin, make sure that you can afford it. If you can't, then simply forget about it for a while. A lesson once every three weeks isn't going to give you the skill levels that you need.

Try to include in your programme a fair number of two-hour lessons. A lot of time is wasted in one-hour sessions. You'll probably waste a few minutes talking, a bit more on adjusting your seat, getting comfortable and so on. And you'll *definitely* spend time on repeating what you did in the last lesson. This means that the number of minutes available for learning new techniques is greatly reduced.

22

As you get closer to the test you should also increase your time in a car to the point where it is almost a daily activity. Indeed, many schools and instructors now offer intensive courses in which you start from zero knowledge and aim to pass at the end of a week. While this can be effective, it can also be a strain. A compromise mixing both types of training is often the best answer.

Quality control

It is generally agreed that in most things, quality is more important than quantity. This applies to learning to drive. Although it is important that you spend as much time in a car as possible, you must also ensure that it is quality time. A factor overlooked by most learners is the time of day you take lessons. It's often easier to slot in training after work or in the early evening. You need to ask yourself, however, whether you are at your best just then. For most of the day you'll have been under pressure from customers, workmates, bosses, and various stressful situations. Your body will be tense, your mind racing, and your attitude lousy. Let's face it – there are better things to do after work than learning to drive. A Chinese proverb states that an hour of instruction before noon is worth two hours after it. Like many proverbs, it contains more than a grain of truth. When you are at your freshest and most relaxed you are likely to be enthusiastic and receptive to learning. Training when you are at your best will save you both time and money. Think about this when you plan your schedule.

It's also important to decide when to book your test. There's little point attempting a morning or midday test if you've only ever practised at night or weekends. Make sure that your training corresponds with the kind of traffic flows and problems that you are likely to encounter in your examination.

The kind of help you don't need

It's only natural that friends and family should want to help you pass your driving test. Those most likely to offer you 'tuition', however, are paradoxically the ones who are likely to cause you the most problems. Years of driving can make people take 'short cuts' with the result that a great many would fail the test if they had to sit it again. Technical errors, over-confidence and sloppiness are going to be offered up to you as 'experience'. Once in your system, any such habits will be as hard to eradicate as a computer virus. If you do go out with other drivers then make sure that they provide genuine accompanied practice rather than cheap instruction.

Look and learn

Keep your eyes and mind open as you stand in bus queues, car parks and so on. There's an awful lot of free lessons to be had simply by watching qualified drivers. Admittedly, most of the information to be had will concern how *not* to behave, but it's valuable nonetheless. Watch carefully how people park and reverse. Try to diagnose what sort of in-car movements are magnified into problems by the vehicle.

Many bad habits relate simply to survival. Paying more attention to the mobile phone than the road, eating or even sleeping at the wheel, parking cars without thought, driving too close to the car in front, etc, can be dangerous habits. Observe these bad habits and cultivate good ones in yourself. After all, it's easier to avoid trouble than it is to get out of it.

Take the wheel

A final word about your preparation for the test. The responsibility for this rests with you and you alone. At the very outset of your development you must see yourself as responsible for both your efforts and actions. Don't be passive about this. Over-reliance on an instructor will lead to the sudden, paralysing terror that grips the candidate just before the test. Be positive, and accept that it is you that has to work, not the instructor.

3

READY TO GO?

The anatomy of fear

Exam nerves can be crippling in the extreme, so it's important that you come to terms with them at the very outset of your training. Every person has his or her own unique set of fears. There are different types of fear. The fear experienced when climbing up a slippery rock face, for instance, is relatively easy to understand. It is to do with the fact that a fall might lead to injury or death. Other fears, however, are a more complex blend of anxieties – and it is this sort of fear that a test can induce. Before you can deal with this fear, it must be broken down into its components. Take a sheet of paper and list why the fear of failing your test is such a big issue. Is it the fear of 'letting down' a partner or a parent? Or is it a fear of being laughed at by friends and peers? Or even that if you pass you will then be expected to drive?

With your list complete, examine each reason in turn. As you do so, you will realize that most of them are illusory or trivial. Put your fears on paper and put them into perspective. The symptoms of fear are very real. When faced with real or imaginary danger, our bodies are changed by the 'fight or flight' response. Adrenaline is pumped into our blood system, breathing becomes faster and more shallow, and the heart rate is increased. It doesn't matter whether the danger we face is a charging rhino or a driving test. You can't avoid these basic reactions, but you can learn to control them and use them.

Slow lane, fast lane

There's a slow lane and a fast lane for test nerves. The slow lane is that which accompanies any sort of examination. As the time draws near individuals worry about their lack of preparation, become tense or angry and occasionally may even develop a physical illness.

Thankfully, most people only suffer from fast lane problems. Trembling, shaking and memory loss that leads to temporary confusion can occur the day or hour before the test. And if a mistake is made in the opening stages, well, it's time to go home isn't it?

With any luck, you will only experience the mildest of worries when you take your test. It's important to realize, however, that worries can play a part in your success or failure. For this reason, it's worthwhile looking at a few techniques that you can use if problems do arise.

Immunize yourself against fear

Immunization works by introducing germs into the body to protect it against diseases. Coping with test nerves involves exactly the same principles.

A driving test can be nerve-wracking because it is an unknown experience. Your own instructor will probably put you through a mock test, but this may not be sufficient. Over the weeks or months that you've been with your instructor, you will have become used to him or her. Even if you're told it's a serious test, it's still not that threatening.

Book yourself a mock test with an instructor other than your own in the run-up to the big day. This should not be done with the aim of acquiring new techniques, but in order to deliberately place yourself in a stressful situation. You should emerge feeling stronger, but if you don't – do it again. In this way you will become accustomed to fear and control your response towards it.

The mock test is possibly the single most valuable precautionary technique you can employ in your efforts to pass. Consider the extra expense to be a kind of insurance policy protecting a major investment.

Picture this

Visualization is the name given to another self-help technique that can help you overcome slow lane test nerves. It works on the simple principle that a person experiencing an illusion can no longer tell the difference between the illusion and reality. Illusion can be very powerful. Exploit it.

There are two main kinds of visualization that you can use to overcome test nerves. The first is often used by sports stars and actors. Pick out a manoeuvre or driving sequence that you find difficult and then close your eyes. Imagine yourself in the car performing the sequence in question in text book fashion and enjoy the positive feeling that goes with it. Repeat this controlled fantasy over and over again until it seems to be the most natural thing in the world. It will be too, when it comes to your test.

The second visualization is designed to make you relax. Picture yourself in a lift that is going to travel deep down into your self. Count down ten floors over a couple of minutes and then see the doors open to reveal your own imagined heaven. It could be a warm, sunny beach or a forest clearing, as long as it's real to you. Cast off your worries like unnecessary clothes and enjoy the peace. When you've had enough, count yourself back 'up' to reality. As the doors open you'll emerge refreshed and relaxed and able to take the test in your stride.

Breathe easy

Eastern religions have long recognized the links between mind and body. As was discussed earlier, fear and alarm bring about physiological changes. The reverse is also true, however: you can use your body to change your state of mind.

Deep or controlled breathing is one of the most obvious ways of dealing with nerves. Use this simple, inconspicuous technique in the minutes leading up to your test.

- Place your thumb over your right nostril and gently suck in air through your left. Take the air in slowly as if you are filling your lungs with water from the bottom up.

- When you can no longer absorb any more air, seal both nostrils for a count of five.

- Open your right nostril and expel the air in a slow, controlled fashion.

- Now draw in the air through the right nostril as you seal your left.

- Exhale through your left nostril then reverse the process. Repeat the cycle four or five times.

Controlled breathing like this will help get extra oxygen to your brain and counteract the changes that fear brings.

Under pressure

Another technique that you can use to steady acute nerves is borrowed from acupressure, which is essentially acupuncture without the needles. Through centuries of experimentation, Chinese scholars observed that applying pressure to certain parts of the body can have dramatic effects on the nervous system.

Locate the spots shown in the diagram overleaf on your own body and apply a gentle kneading pressure with the knuckle of your first finger. This may take a little practice, but when you find the right spot you'll feel the effect. Breathe freely as you apply the pressure and think pleasant, calm and relaxing thoughts.

Doctor's orders

Many learner drivers consult their doctor for 'something to get them through the test'. Often disguised as a request for tranquilizers to overcome sleeplessness, this approach to driving is fraught with danger. Aside from the fact that these drugs will slow down vital reaction times, they won't increase your skill or knowledge. Are you really saying that you can only drive if doped?

If you suffer from excessive nerves, nausea or sleeplessness, then step back a bit and ask yourself what's really going on. Postpone your test and examine your motivation and training record. First and foremost, do you really want to drive, or are you going along with someone else's

31

Points to relieve anxiety, fear or restlessness

Press quite hard with tip of finger in these places;
rotate the tip of finger to stimulate the point

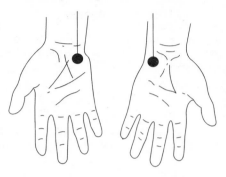

Same action applies to these points; apply pressure to
points on both left and right hands in turn

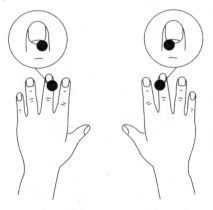

wishes? Should this be the case, then talk the problem through with that person. Anyone who cares for you isn't likely to force you into an activity that makes you physically sick. If, on the other hand, you do want to drive, then try the alternative methods listed above, or join a yoga or Tai Chi class to help you relax.

Finally, as mentioned earlier, examine your training patterns. Sporadic instruction, where every lesson you seem to be 'starting again', is no good for anyone's confidence. Experiment with the duration of your lessons and when you do them. Sustained activity, not medicines, will sort out your nerves. You should avoid taking substances of any sort before a test. Spend your money on tuition or relaxation based activities instead.

No pain, no gain

If you go to the gym it may hurt. If you go to the dentist it may hurt. If you take a test you will probably experience nerves. Accept this as a fact and it won't seem half so bad. Keep training!

4

CHANGING GEAR

The spice of driving life

Learning to drive can be pretty boring at times. When the novelty wears off and routines have to be practised again and again, concentration and motivation can suffer. A good instructor will help enliven the process, but you can help by putting the spice back into driving with a little variety.

Learning a new skill follows a definite pattern. Initial rapid progress gives way to less dramatic development as the learning curve flattens out. It's at this point you need to vary your routines so that you can absorb knowledge in new and fun ways. Be like a weight-trainer who 'hits' the same muscle from different angles with a selection of exercises.

There are many kinds of supplementary training that you can add to your diet. Quite a few of them relate to driving theory, which you probably thought you'd finished with after passing your written examination. That's a mistake which is commonly made.

Theory and practice

Far too many people think they have finished with theory after passing the required test. Such an attitude betrays a lack of understanding about theory and practice. The principles you learn at this stage need to stay with you for as long as you are driving. Ignore the basics and very soon you are going to get into trouble. A sound grasp of principles is the foundation of good technique.

Off the shelf

An obvious place to begin your quest for knowledge to help you pass your test is at your local library or bookshop. Some books, such as the DSA publications listed in Appendix 1, are almost essential to your progress, and you should definitely read, if not own these. To buy them is an investment, not an extravagant purchase, because you'll be able to use them all your life. Besides these DSA publications, there are lots of other books on motoring that are worth your attention. You should try and read as many of these as possible. Even if one piece of information you have read sticks with you, you will have profited greatly. Set aside some time every week to read up on driving skills and practice. Soak up knowedge rather than cramming it in. Your aim is not to become a bookworm or know-all, but someone with a sound grasp of what driving is all about.

On the box

Apart from books on motoring, which can be seen as essential to your progress, another way to boost your understanding is through the use of the television set.

Instructional videos are an excellent and inexpensive way to beef up your training. You should also look out for the occasional series on television which show you know NOT to drive by illustrating all sorts of irresponsible behaviour and its consequences. Learn to do better.

On line

If you have access to a computer, then it too can be pressed into service for the test. A number of driving-related programmes are available, with more sure to come on the market every year. You could, if you wished, work on these on those days or nights when you are unable to drive a real car.

Got it taped?

Instructional tapes such as *The Driving Test Talks Back* can be bought from any large bookshop or from your instructor. A taped *How To Drive* series can also give you a new way of learning techniques that might have become over-familiar or boring.

Inspirational tapes are filled with up-beat messages to increase motivation. Some are presented by 'star' names or hypnotherapists. If you suffer badly from nerves or blocks to learning, consider buying one of these.

Fun and games

You might have played board or computer-based educational games in the run up to your theory test. If you did, and have put them away, then dig them out again. If you didn't, consider acquiring some. Games of this sort can help instill driving principles in a painless and fun manner. In

37

the weeks running up to the test they also contribute to your sense of total immersion in the goal. Your sense of commitment needs to be absolute and undiluted, and games can complement your practical training.

Ask your instructor about any games or quizzes that might be of benefit to you. If you don't want to spend money on games, then try to 'outguess' a friend with situations that you are likely to encounter on the road.

Try teaching

One of the best ways of learning any new skill is to try teaching it to someone else. No longer are you a passive recipient of knowledge, but you are 'in charge' of what's going on. All of a sudden you have to concentrate and explain the reason for what you are doing, rather than just mindlessly repeating it.

To begin with, select a topic or procedure that you are comfortable with. Read up on it as fully as you can from several sources, and make notes of the most important points involved. At this stage, enlist the help of a friend who holds a licence. Explain that you do not want to be taught, but that you want to 'instruct' for your own good so that you can learn the approved drill by heart. This can be done on or off the road, but however you choose to do it, do it by the book. Exercises like this are also useful in that they encourage a positive and active approach to learning. Don't become too dependent on your instructor. Think and act for yourself.

Pass notes

You can either buy ready-made pass notes, or make your own. The point of these cards is to have a quick-reference

written record of the key elements of specific driving procedures. Making your own cards has the added benefit of
(a) involving you in research and (b) fixing the information
in your memory by the act of making the cards. They don't
need to be too elaborate or flash; just write out what you
need to know in bullet-point fashion.

Stay hungry

Have you ever noticed that when you are doing something
that you enjoy the time flies? Or that it drags when you are
doing something that is boring or of no interest to you? At
the outset of your training everything was new and exciting,
and because of that learning was fun. Later in the cycle,
you may come to feel that you know everything that you
need to know already. To get the most out of lessons, treat
each one as if it was the first. Stay hungry and keen for
information and learning will stay fun.

5

IGNITION

Last minute preparations

As the big day approaches, there are various things that you should check. The precautions listed below may sound obvious, but an amazing number of people fail their tests each year because of them.

In the week before the test you need to be certain that the following conditions are fulfilled:

- That you know where your provisional licence is. Hunting around for it on the day is not recommended.

- That your licence is *signed*.

- That you know exactly when and where your test is to be held. Ask your instructor to write this down.

- That your instructor knows when and where to pick you up. Ask your instructor to write this down.

Care and maintenance

Do's and don'ts:

- *Do* concentrate your resources in the week before the test. Avoid late nights, wild parties and excessive alcohol.

- *Do* have a full breakfast or lunch prior to the test.

- *Do* make sure that you have enough time to get ready in a relaxed fashion.

- *Don't* watch the news on television, or read papers. Listen to music or read a good book instead.

- *Don't* panic.

Dress sense

A piece of modern folklore that relates only to female learner drivers says that a short skirt is almost certain to guarantee a pass with a male examiner. This is absolute rubbish of course, though it is surprising how many people believe it to be the truth. Having said that, there are ways in which your dress sense can marginally influence the outcome of your test.

Driving examiners are human beings with the same emotions, prejudices and assumptions as the rest of us. They too make split-second decisions on whether they like a person or not. Decisions that can be coloured by how people dress and conduct themselves for a very serious test. If, for example, you were interviewing, would you opt for the person who came smartly dressed or the one who looked scruffy? Appearances matter.

Dress as though you mean business and give the examiner every chance to 'buy' you as a safe and responsible driver. To elaborate: the most exprensive designer outfit in the world won't make an examiner pass you if you're a bad driver, nor will unsuitable clothing make for a fail if you're good. If, however, your case is marginal, then subjective influences might just have some influence on where a tick is placed.

On a more practical level, dress to allow yourself freedom of movement. Should you have long hair, ensure that it is tied back and will not distract you. Pay attention to your footwear, too, and try to wear the shoes that you have trained in.

Visual awareness

Intense concentration on a task has its down side. The eyes tend to become fixed on a particular point in space with the result that the rest of the world goes out of focus. Inexperienced drivers are especially prone to this symptom, and it contributes to several kinds of test failure.

During the weeks before your test, practise visual scanning exercises, moving your eyes from one area of the road to another quite rapidly. Try to take in a complete picture of what is going on around you.

Two weeks before your test, make sure that you can read a number plate at the required distance.

Routine service

The word 'routine' tends to have connotations of being dull and boring. However, routine can literally be a lifesaver. A regular drill can help a driver switch on to an alert and appropriate mindset. It can have practical advantages too. Make a ritual of adjusting mirrors, seats and so on every time you get in the car as though switching on instruments in your brain. The routine will help calm you in the instant before the test commences.

Countdown

Ten points to bear in mind as you prepare for the test:

10. You *must* be good enough for the test. No responsible instructor is going to risk possible action by the DSA through entering students who are not fully trained.

9. Nerves are normal. Fears and worries are normal. Do not convince yourself that you are useless, incapable or doomed because you experience these emotions.

8. Accept that test failure isn't a matter of life and death. You can take your test time and time again providing you have the patience and money. Relax and do the best you can.

7. Be prepared physically, mentally and emotionally to sit another test within a short space of time if so required.

6. Make sure that you are physically comfortable. Do not wear clothes that might make you over-hot or restrict your movement. Visit a toilet before the test.

5. Breathe deeply and slowly. Use your body to control your mind and emotions.

4. Remember that the examiner isn't there to trick or trap you. He or she will not ask you to do anything that you have not already done many times before.

3. Ensure that the car seat, mirrors, etc, are adjusted to your liking.

2. Remember that you are *not* a passenger. You will need to make prompt and positive decisions.

1. If you make a mistake don't despair. Expect to make minor faults, and remember that the odd mistake or two does not mean the End of Civilization As We Know It. Adopt a mature attitude and keep driving to the best of your ability.

On failing your test

The next chapter is entirely devoted to the subject of test failure, but before that here are a few practical notes. On hearing that you have failed, don't storm out of the car, burst into tears or display any other sign of immaturity, or, for that matter, get angry with the examiner. Instead, take it as an accepted fact that you did not perform the actions you should have done exactly as required. Put some distance between yourself and what has happened. The examiner was evaluating your driving ability, not your worth as a human being.

Ask the examiner quietly and politely why you failed. If your attitude is non-aggressive then he or she may offer some useful insights. And don't tear up your failure sheet either! This document will be useful to both yourself and your instructor – on it the examiner has written down your weak points. Learn from it: use it as a tool to ensure you will pass the next time round. Ripping it into shreds might be fun, but it isn't rational. The people who designed the car that you are hoping to drive will have had similar reports condemning their work and efforts. They didn't throw them away without a second glance; they used them to correct their errors.

You can, of course, dispute the outcome of your test as far as you wish. You can argue prejudice, foul play, inconsistency or whatever you like. You can take it up with the DSA, your MP, or whoever. But frankly, you aren't going to get very far. Those who might be able to offer expert judgement weren't in the car, and there is little that can be offered in the way of evidence against most cases. Put your anger to more positive uses: turn it into resolve to improve those points upon which you failed. And remember: overcoming failure begins by accepting it.

6

REPAIRS

Emergency stop

More than fifty per cent of those sitting their test on any given day are going to fail it. Realistically, you could be one of those people in spite of all your efforts and expense. There are effective responses to this situation, but before you can implement them you must come to terms with the emotional consequences of a negative outcome. This begins with changing your attitude towards failure.

A positive view of failure

How you feel about what has happened to you is obviously going to dictate your practical response to it. If you hold failure to be a crushing blow, then this will only heighten your tension on the next attempt. If, on the other hand, you have a positive outlook towards failure then it will be at worst an irritation, at best a challenge.

They key to this process is to replace bad thoughts about failure with positive thoughts about failure. It's about seeing a glass as being half full rather than half empty.

Study these attitudes towards failure and reprogramme your personal 'on-board' computer with them. Do this until you believe them and you will snatch victory out of the jaws of defeat:

- **Failure is part of the learning process**

  Failure is a natural part of the learning process and as such is not to be despised or derided. Unless an individual is very lucky or very talented, he or she is going to take a few tumbles when coming to grips with any new activity. It doesn't matter whether that activity is learning to ski, to dance or to drive: the pattern always stays the same. Repeated attempts and failures to master a skill lead to eventual success. You just have to learn to roll with the blows, knowing that you'll win in the end.

- **Failure is what you say it is**

  Passing your test isn't the only yardstick that you should measure your efforts by. Most of the human race, past, present or future, are incapable of doing what you have done already. It may not seem like it on a busy road, but only a small fraction of the population can drive. In learning to handle a car you have already achieved a great deal, and you should not belittle that achievement. All that is required of you is the staying power and diligence to apply yourself to passing the test.

- **Failure is possible only when you stop trying**

  Until you tear up your provisional licence, swear that you are never going to drive and mean it, you cannot call yourself a failure. Up to that point you are a student, and students are expected to make mistakes: that is why they are called students, and not masters! What you are really doing by branding yourself as a 'failure' is taking the easy way out. You're saying that you can no longer be bothered to make an effort to study or accept a little criticism. If you did that in your hobby, your job or relationships, you wouldn't get very far.

- **Success is judged on outcome**
  When Edison strove to invent the light bulb his attempts failed hundreds and hundreds of times. In the end, however, he did make it work, and we remember that success, rather than all the failed attempts he under-went. It's the same with any athlete or sportsman or woman. We judge them not by the number of failed attempts they make, but on their successful attempts. In competing or playing, they are taking a chance, giving it their best shot. If they didn't risk failure, then they wouldn't have the chance to break that world record or score that unforgettable goal. Nothing ventured, nothing gained. Nobody is counting failed attempts but you. Concentrate on the outcome rather than the process – the reward of having the licence will overshadow the history behind it.

- **Failure is keeping me alive**
  There is a very big difference between failing a French exam (for example) and failing the driving test. A failure of the French exam is not a matter of life and death, whereas, at the bottom line, failing a driving test is a matter of keeping you and other road users alive. Examiners fail people not because of trivial details, but because they need to prevent injury and death at the hands of unskilled drivers. By indicating that you are not quite ready to go solo, your examiner is preserving

your life and the lives of others. You should be grateful for such advice and not angry about it.

The attitudes described above will give you a more positive outlook on failure. Before moving on to practical measures, however, there is one other demon that needs to be exorcised.

Changing instructors

When something goes wrong it's natural that you should want to blame someone else for it. However, if you've selected your instructor according to the principles outlined earlier (see page 14), then switching would be futile. The instruction you have received will have been competent, capable and correct. Only one person can put it into practice though. You.

Examine your performance in detail. Did you apply everything that you had been taught? Did you follow the procedures that you had practised, or did you try to improvise? Be honest with yourself before you go to the expense and inconvenience of starting all over again.

Mind games

Failure strikes at both your self-confidence and your motivation. After repeated failures, you don't really want to get back in that car, do you? You know that you need to go back to work on your driving, but you don't actually *feel* that you want to. Until this is sorted out, you will be wasting both time and money on further instruction.

If your mind is full of worries and negative thoughts then this will interfere with your performance. You are programmed for failure. The techniques that follow are designed to help you change your mental attitudes. Experiment and be prepared to let go of your need to fail.

Affirmation cards

Affirmation cards are a cheap and effective way of changing your attitude. Buy a small packet of index cards and a plastic wallet that can hold twenty-one of them. Write out on a sheet of paper twenty-one positive statements about driving or what driving can do for you, for example:

● I can drive already; I just need to pass a short test.

● Soon I won't have to take the train to work every morning.

● Regular practice will lead to success every time.

● Reading this is making me a better driver.

Having decided on your statements, you then need to transfer them to the cards. The final step is to read through your collection twenty-one times a day. This can be at bus stops, in spare moments or whatever. Constant repetition is the key; the ideas need to sink down into your subconscious mind to replace the negative and angry ones lodged down there.

Bonus points

The concept that a job well done merits a reward is drummed into us from childhood onwards – whether it's a gold star from the teacher or a bonus from our employer. We expect to see our effort and achievement recognized. When it isn't, we feel both cheated and disappointed. This principle can work for you as you prepare for your test.

How about making a list of treats or rewards – things you would like to own (a CD perhaps) or do (see a show). Then, when you reach your goal – you conquer your reverse park or master the three-point turn – you can reward yourself with something from the list.

Video plus

Instructional videos are not the only ones that can help you pass your test. Your favourite 'feel good' films can also help you to have a more positive attitude to life. The familiar but potent messages from these films can help you feel better about yourself and so prepare you to perform to the best of your ability when the big day comes, and of course the videos will help you relax if you watch them in the run up to your test.

Hypnotherapy

Throughout your formal training you've had the guidance, companionship and concern of a personal tutor next to you. At the moment of the test, however, you are suddenly deprived of this person who may have been with you since you first learnt how to start the car. Small wonder, then, that you feel vulnerable and in need of a comforting voice?

Hypnotherapy has been shown to provide that reassuring voice when in the grip of an acute fear or phobia. This kind of hypnotherapy takes place over two or three sessions and is designed to embed positive attitudes in your subconscious mind. The cost of a few sessions of this sort is minimal compared to its possible benefits, and could be worth considering.

Aromatherapy

Aromatherapy is a technique that uses scents and oils to treat particular conditions associated with the mind and body. Practitioners claim that fears, phobias and stress can be eased by the correct application of these substances.

Your secret weapon

Your secret weapon in the war against test nerves is . . . *Enthusiasm*. Enthusiasm will turn failure into experience. Enthusiasm will put all your problems into perspective and make you look for the next challenge. Enthusiasm is a wonderful thing.

Most of us tend to be rather half-hearted about life and take what we've got for granted. And yet, on the whole, we are so very, very lucky. Your life may not be as wonderful as it might yet be, but compared to what the vast majority of humanity has to put up with it's pretty good. Accept what you've got and be enthusiastic about it! This will take a little practice, but it can be developed if you work hard. Learn to rediscover the enthusiasm that you felt on first getting your provisional licence, on passing your theory test, on completing a good lesson. Get that back and you'll find taking the test again no problem at all.

7

STOP . . .
PASS . . . GO

Driven to tears

Qualified motorists often tell non-qualified motorists that you learn to drive *after* you've passed your test. In one sense this is absolutely correct. Removed from an artificial situation in which your instructor can slam on the brakes if problems arise, you are on your own. As you encounter darkness, fog, ice and motorways you will discover that there is still an awful lot you don't know about driving. Experience, of course, is a great teacher – if you survive it, that is. Regrettably, a lot of new drivers don't. They get killed or maimed.

Many people believe that learning to drive is a one-off event like a twenty-first birthday. They believe their driving is perfect. They even have a bit of paper to prove it. The reality of the situation is different. That's because learning to drive isn't an event but a process.

A lifeskills approach to driving

Driving isn't merely a case of passing a test, it's about doing things in a safe and sensible manner. About staying alive.

Think about driving for a moment and compare it to the other activities in your life. If you went to a gym regularly and then stopped, would you expect to remain as fit and shapely? If you played a musical instrument for a while and then dropped practising, would you expect to be able to play to the same standard? Driving is exactly the same – a skill that develops with practice, and diminishes without it.

First things

After passing your driving test you should book some more lessons with an approved driving instructor. Your chances of injury or death as a newly-qualified driver are much greater than for any other group. You have a licence, but it is unlikely that you will have had the experience of hazardous conditions awaiting you in the real world. Book some time with your instructor in the months after your test to get to grips with these problems. Remember the old adage that still applies even in a metric world: an ounce of prevention is worth a pound of cure.

Moving targets

Nor should you be merely content with learning how to drive safely at night or in bad weather. There are many ways in which you can expand and develop your skills as a motorist. The first and most obvious course of action is to train as an Advanced Driver. Courses offered by The

Institute of Advanced Motorists (see Appendix Two) will not only help you to sharpen your talents, they will bring tangible benefits.

You may want to develop skills that are associated with driving. For example, you might want to do First Aid training or basic repair classes, to prepare yourself for unexpected situations. Some police authorities run short courses on coping with road rage or safe driving practice for women on their own. If you want to be more adventurous, you could drive a tank or an amphibious vehicle at one of the off-road centres around the country. The key thing is to continue to develop.

You should also think about booking another test every few years. European law may eventually make this compulsory. Nobody thinks twice about having regular check-ups with their dentist or optician, nor about putting their car in for its MOT. Checking on your driving technique is no less important. Experience can bring with it over-confidence, sloppiness and bad habits. Book a mock test with your old instructor and ask to be put through the mill. None of this is compulsory, of course – but wouldn't you like to be a better than average driver?

The road ahead

Your driving test isn't the end of your progress, but just a beginning. Take a lifeskills approach to driving, and seek to improve your abilities by whatever means are open to you. You'll be a better motorist for the effort.

APPENDIX 1

Listed below is a selection of books that are useful for every stage of your driving life. Some are test-oriented, some are more advanced, and some are aimed at overcoming psychological barriers and fears.

HMSO (1997) *The Driving Test*, HMSO, Norwich.
 If you fail your test without having read this first, then you have nobody to blame but yourself. It is absolutely essential reading.

HMSO (1997) *The Highway Code*, HMSO, Norwich.
 Essential reading.

Lambert, D, and The Diagram Group (1995) *Driving Skills*, Harper Collins, London.
 A chunky, pocket-sized guide ideal for reading in spare moments. Well-illustrated and succinct.

Yule, G (1996) *Behind The Wheel*, Otter Publications.
 Sections on theory and practical skills make this book doubly useful. Recommended.

Stacey, M (1998) *How to Drive in Ten Easy Lessons*, Kogan Page, London.
  This book has served generations of learners and will doubtless continue to do so. Buy or borrow then read it.

HMSO, *The Driver's Manual*, HMSO, Norwich.
  This is one of the set texts for those wanting to become driving instructors, so it's no surprise that it is packed with technical information. A well-illustrated book of use throughout your driving lifetime.

The Police Federation (1994) *Roadcraft*, HMSO, Norwich.
  If you seriously want to become an advanced driver then you need to master the contents of this, the police driver's manual.

Topper, T, *Very Advanced Driving*, Elliot Right Way Books.
  A useful addition to the shelves, this is a short but nonetheless valuable work on the subject of better motor skills.

Wiseman, J (1997) *The SAS Driving Survival Manual*, Harper Collins, London.
  Lofty Wiseman is best known for the teaching of jungle craft to the SAS. In this book he has turned his attention to the business of surviving on the roads. Dealing with items as basic as repairs or procedure to possible incidents such as road rage and accidents, it is a book that might one day save your life.

APPENDIX 2

The ability to drive is a 'life skill', something which can develop, expand and change long after your test. There are things that you can do with your life skill which will improve your insurability, employability, or survival: there are things that you can do with it that are simply fun! Listed below are a few of the possible options that you might want to explore.

Tests

The Advanced Driving Test

The Advanced Driving Test is something that most people have heard of. Probably the most difficult and respected qualification of its kind in the world, it can have real insurance and job implications. The single most important thing about it, however, is that IAM members have a 50 to 70 per cent lower accident rate than other members of the driving community. This is in part to do with extra training, and in part due to the different attitude towards driving that it brings. Further information from: The Institute of Advanced Motorists, IAM House, 359 Chiswick High Road, London W4 4HS; Tel. 0181 994 4403.

The RoSPA Advanced Driving Test

The Royal Society for the Prevention of Accidents also conducts its own advanced driving tests throughout the UK. These result in gold, silver and bronze certificates, which provide a real incentive to keep training and keep improving. Further information from: The Administrations Officer, RoSPA Advanced Drivers Association, Cannon House, The Priory, Birmingham B4 6BS; Tel. 0121 200 2461.

Fun

If you feel the need for adventure and speed, get it off the road rather than on it! The following companies offer you the chance to drive everything from racing cars to tanks, in addition to things like skid patches, which can also have practical applications.

The Everyman Driving Centre, Mallory Park Circuit, Leics, LE9 7QE; Tel. 01455 841670.
Racing cars, Ferraris, tanks, LGVs, etc!

Phil Price Rally School, Coed Harbour, Llangunlla, Knighton, Powys LD7 1TD; Tel. 01547 550300.
Rally driving in authentic conditions.

Silverstone Rally School, Silverstone Park, Northants, NN12 1TD; Tel. 01327 857413.
Skid control, handbrake turns and more on a gravel special stage.

Ian Taylor, Ian Taylor Motor Racing School, Thruxton Circuit, Andover, Hants, SP11 8PW.
   Single seat racing cars, MGF sports cars etc.

Jim Russell Racing Drivers School, Donnington Park, Castle Donnington, Derby, D74 2RD; Tel. 01332 811430.
   Single seaters, touring cars, 4×4s and Skid School,